A STORY
A STORY

AN AFRICAN TALE RETOLD AND ILLUSTRATED BY
GAIL E. HALEY

AN ALADDIN BOOK
Atheneum

This book is for Marguerite, and all her
brothers and sisters, both black and white,
and especially for Arnold, with all my love

Many African stories, whether or not they are about Kwaku Ananse the "spider man," are called "Spider Stories." This book is about how that came to be.

"Spider stories" tell how small, defenseless men or animals outwit others and succeed against great odds. These stories crossed the Atlantic Ocean in the cruel ships that delivered slaves to the Americas. Their descendants still tell some of these stories today. Ananse has become Anancy in the Caribbean isles, while he survives as "Aunt Nancy" in the southern United States.

You will find many African words in this story. If you listen carefully, you can tell what they mean by their sounds. At times words and phrases are repeated several times. Africans repeat words to make them stronger. For example: "So small, so small, so small," means very, very, very small.

The African storyteller begins:

"We do not really mean, we do not really mean that what we are about to say is true. A story, a story; let it come, let it go."

Once, oh small children
round my knee, there were no
stories on earth to
hear. All the stories belonged
to Nyame, the Sky God.
He kept them in a golden box
next to his royal stool.

Ananse, the Spider man, wanted
to buy the Sky God's stories.
So he spun a web up to the sky.

When the Sky God heard what Ananse
wanted, he laughed: "Twe, twe, twe.
The price of my stories is that you
bring me Osebo the leopard of-
the-terrible-teeth, Mmboro the hornet
who-stings-like-fire, and Mmoatia
the fairy whom-men-never-see."

Ananse bowed and answered:
"I shall gladly pay the price."

"Twe, twe, twe," chuckled the Sky God.
"How can a weak old man like you,
so small, so small, so small, pay my
price?"

But Ananse merely climbed down
to earth to find the
things that the Sky God demanded.

Ananse ran along the jungle path—
yiridi, yiridi, yiridi—till he came
to Osebo the leopard-of-the-terrible-teeth.

"Oho, Ananse," said the leopard,
"you are just in time to be my lunch."

Ananse replied: "As for that, what will
happen will happen. But first let us play
the binding binding game."

The leopard, who was fond of games,
asked: "How is it played?"

"With vine creepers," explained Ananse.
"I will bind you by your foot and foot.
Then I will untie you, and you can tie me up."

"Very well," growled the leopard,
who planned to eat Ananse
as soon as it was his turn to bind him.

So Ananse tied the leopard
by his foot
by his foot
by his foot
by his foot, with the vine creeper.
Then he said: "Now, Osebo,
you are ready to meet the Sky God."
And he hung the tied leopard
in a tree in the jungle.

Next Ananse cut a frond from a banana tree and filled a calabash with water. He crept through the tall grasses, sora, sora, sora, till he came to the nest of Mmboro, the hornets-who-sting-like-fire.

Ananse held the banana leaf over his head as an umbrella. Then he poured some of the water in the calabash over his head.

The rest he emptied over the hornet's nest
and cried: "It is raining, raining, raining.
Should you not fly into my calabash, so
that the rain will not tatter your wings?"

"Thank you. Thank you," hummed the hornets,
and they flew into the calabash—fom!
Ananse quickly stopped the mouth of the gourd.

"Now, Mmbora, you are ready to meet the Sky God,"
said Ananse. And he hung the calabash full
of hornets onto the tree next to the leopard.

Ananse now carved
a little wooden doll holding
a bowl. He covered the doll
from top to bottom with sticky
latex gum. Then he filled the
doll's bowl with pounded yams.

He set the little doll at the
foot of a flamboyant tree where
fairies like to dance. Ananse
tied one end of a vine round
the doll's head and, holding
the other end in his hand,
he hid behind a bush.

In a little while, Mmoatia the
fairy-whom-no-man-sees came
dancing, dancing, dancing, to the
foot of the flamboyant tree.
There she saw the doll holding
the bowl of yams.

Mmoatia said: "Gum baby, I am hungry. May I eat some of your yams?"

Ananse pulled at the vine in his hiding place, so that the doll seemed to nod its head. So the fairy took the bowl from the doll and ate all the yams.

"Thank you, Gum baby," said the fairy.
But the doll did not answer.

"Don't you reply when I thank you?"
cried the angered fairy.
The doll did not stir.

"Gum baby, I'll slap your crying place
unless you answer me,"
shouted the fairy. But the wooden doll
remained still and silent.
So the fairy slapped her crying place
—pa! Her hand stuck
fast to the gum baby's sticky cheek.

"Let go of my hand, or I'll
slap you again."—Pa! She slapped
the doll's crying place with
her other hand. Now the fairy was
stuck to the gum baby with
both hands, and she was furious. She
pushed against the doll with
her feet, and they also stuck fast.

Now Ananse came out of hiding.
"You are ready to meet the Sky God,
Mmoatia." And he carried
her to the tree where the leopard
and the hornets were waiting.

Ananse spun a web round Osebo,
Mmboro, and Mmoatia.
Then he spun a web to the sky.
He pulled up his captives
behind him, and set them down
at the feet of the Sky God.

"O, Nyame," said Ananse, bowing low,
"here is the price
   you ask for your stories:
   Osebo the leopard-of-the-terrible-
   teeth, Mmboro the hornets-
   who-sting-like-fire, and Mmoatia
   the fairy-whom-men-never-see."

Nyame the Sky God called together all
the nobles of his court and
addressed them in a loud voice:
"Little Ananse, the spider man,
   has paid me the price I ask for my
   stories. Sing his praise. I command you."

"From this day and going
   on forever," proclaimed the Sky God,
"my stories belong to Ananse and shall
   be called 'Spider Stories.'"

"Eeeee, Eeeee, Eeeee,"
   shouted all the assembled nobles.

So Ananse took the golden box of
stories back to earth, to the people of his
village. And when he opened the box
all the stories scattered to the
corners of the world, including this one.

This is my story which I have related. If it be sweet, or if it be not sweet, take some elsewhere, and let some come back to me.